The Bunker in the Parsley Fields

Winner of the Iowa Poetry Prize

The Bunker

Poems by Gary Gildner

in the Parsley Fields

University of Iowa Press Ψ Iowa City

University of Iowa Press,

Iowa City 52242

Copyright © 1997 by

Gary Gildner

All rights reserved

Printed in the United States

of America

Design by Richard Hendel

http://www.uiowa.edu/~uipress

Library of Congress

Cataloging-in-Publication Data

Gildner, Gary.

   The bunker in the parsley fields: poems /

by Gary Gildner.

      p.   cm.—(Iowa poetry prize)

   ISBN 0-87745-587-2 (paper)

   I. Title. II. Series.

PS3557.I343B86   1997

811'.54—dc21   96-49449

                                       CIP

01 00   P 5 4 3 2

Printed on acid-free paper

FOR ELIZABETH, MARGARET, & GRETCHEN

Contents

Acknowledgments

Certain poems herein have been previously published, as follows: *Adrienne Lee Press*, "Dear Friends"; *The Ark*, "Cinders"; *Calapooya Collage*, "Jury Duty" and "One Bright Autumn" (originally titled "Lucky"); *Centennial Review*, "In Puerto Rico, She Says"; *Cimarron Review*, "In St. Peter's Home for Nuns" and "Delicately in Small Measure"; *Colorado State Review*, "My Polish Grandfather"; *Cutbank*, "A Dream in the Carpathians"; *Field*, "The Bunker in the Parsley Fields" and "Picked Out a Toka, a Stanley"; *Forkroads*, "A Late Detail from the Depression"; *Georgia Review*, "Close to Trees," "Song: One Summer Afternoon in the Country," and "On Certain Cold Days"; *Limberlost Press*, "A Lullaby"; *The MacGuffin*, "The Sister"; *New Letters*, "In the Garden with Margaret" and "The Stone"; *Northwest Review*, "Lavina" and "Umbels"; *Orpheus* (Bulgaria), "The Sister" and "In the Garden with Margaret"; *Poetry Northwest*, "The Cougar," "Dogtoothed Violets," "Flicker," "Collecting Cowpies," and "Sunday Morning: Marilee Combs Her Red Hair"; *The Prose Poem*, "The Wolverine"; *Shenandoah*, "The Swing" and "Prayer"; and *Witness*, "The Trail."

Part One

The Swing

When you are going well
you hear waves in this rope, and wind,
but no thunder or icy leaves.
No slapping rain. Waves—
and a hum, yes,
as if from a hymn
imperfectly remembered. To bless
everything with—or nothing at all.
Certainly there are no groans
about money or the lack of luck—the moans
of love, maybe, when it comes to that—
sailing out, sailing back.

Cinders

I learned to scoop up grounders on the cinders
in the alley where the grapevines died,
bouncing the ball off Mr. Russian's old chinchilla
hutches that he hauled out there when no one
made him rich and let him quit the night shift—
where every April tiny Mrs. Russian burned
his factory shoes inside a barrel, poking at them
with a stick and saying that she hated her.
I always waited till she wiped her hands
before I fixed my cap and stepped onto the field.
Crouching low like Pee Wee or the Scooter I'd let fly
a smash against the middle hutch and take it
on the short hop, twisting quick to underhand it
softly off the engine block and toss the runner
out by half a step. I could cover territory no one
dared, said Mr. Russian, sometimes watching
with his coffee cup and cheering hard for me
to knock the hutches over. "Damn them all!"
he'd shout, slamming at the fence no grapes
would ever flower on, no jam or wine. He said,
"The ground, by God, is sapped. And where's the little man!"
Then he'd disappear and pound on something
with his hammer. Often I could hear him singing too,
and that's when Mrs. Russian sang along, small and jerky
off somewhere inside the house—*oh I will give you
silver and I will give you gold . . .*
But all through March and early April I was usually
on my own, and learning two important things:

never turn your head and never, never alibi
a flub—if a cinder caused the ball to squib away
you had to shake it off and knuckle down.
All through March and early April I scooped
grounders on the cinders in the alley Mr. Russian
said was mine, the world went away and left it to me.
Letting fly, staying low, and holding out
the smooth, spit-polished pocket of my mitt
I took it.

Playing Catch with My Daughter

I remember the walnuts
uncurling, the lilacs on call,
the day's sweet revolution
and verdurous smell.
I had just cut the grass.
And yes,
when she kicked out
and followed through
all that green day,
how the little spears flew.

Jury Duty

"Please be seated," says the judge
and then that stretch of time
when all the lawyers (six,
in sober business suits that fit)
arrange their papers on a table:
a long finely whorled oak that once
sent feathery green buds
into the world, to announce spring, a brimming
river, lovers, hope, a simple
inevitable story we can only quicken by,
can only weigh by holding
still—listening hard to a cardinal's
call, or a cricket's, or to those
green buds curling out till they come
simply down, sounding
against our feet like the sea washing up
or like nothing but what
they've always been, fall after fall
among bee balm and bluet and the horned fruit
of common devil's-claw along the river.

2

Taking turns the lawyers tell how
this story should go, and it goes
more or less like a river, picking up bright

foil and greasy tins, ferns, twigs,
tangled fishing tackle.
The room is warm. I can smell
a gravel bank, its musky fishbone
litter, the rank and file
of drift and snag . . .

A long time ago I held out a stick
to a turtle, a snapper. I raised her up
by the mouth and out slipped
a perfect egg. I don't think
she was quite ready, and yet
there we were in the muck,
stuck with ourselves
over a stick
—the one too amazed to let go,
the other too angry.

3

"What's true?" a lawyer verging
on tears wants to know. He's asking
the librarian, me, the retired
secretary, the old Navy vet who coughs
and coughs and still, on our breaks,
can't quit smoking. Ashamed
I left the turtle alone.
An ash-colored black man eased

into his pail, fixing a bullhead
to his hands, a pair of pliers,
showing me how you pull
that spiky skin off.
I could hear it
suck and rip. "What's true?"
the lawyer whines again, producing
a long red bandana to blow
his nose. I don't know.
One day I found a wedding
ring in the river. Next day
a baby shoe.

4

At noon we break
for lunch and I take
my apple and cheese and cross
the railroad tracks.
I ease among hawkweed, bristly
broom, some dusty flowering
spurge whose poisonous milky
juice oozes in the sun.
Here by the river
hobos have left their ashes—
a pair of charred sticks
shaped like Y's,
like crutches,

like those bones you find
only in northern pike. Such
nasty-tempered fish and such
delicate wishbones.
I remember one
who slammed like a bully
into my bait from the shadows.
All day I had been happy
under the sun,
sitting quietly beside
my small daughter, watching her
watch her line make ever widening
dreamy circles over that
still placid water.

5

That early spring our daughter was born
we lived on a lake you could not see across,
but soon you could see geese and ducks
coming up from the south and going over
in their sleek formations,
and you could imagine going
with them, the Giant Canada
and specklebelly, the wild, the blue
calling *ha-lonk, ha-lonk*, calling *wah, wahaa*
and among them the pintails and teals
and softly mewing redheads

darting and courting.
Snow still lay on the ground, deep enough
to catch us, and falling back
again and again, breathless,
we beat our wings all up and down
that shore, her mother and I,
telling the child on our breasts
we were flying.

Song: One Summer Afternoon in the Country

when all for a moment is still

and mother stands in the batter's box
and father stands on the hill.

When there is no pain.
When there are no distractions
but the slow shiftings of shade.

When the ball he brings forward now
floats and floats. When she swings.

When over his head. When over the heads
of the two little girls sitting beyond,

their shocked pigtails pointing out
the four known directions. When over
the rhubarb patch and over the scraggly

kid goat tolling his bell
more or less—to signal not so much

the ball sailing over everyone
but the simple lifting up

of a ripe dandelion
he might chew on.
When over the fading snow fence

they haven't disturbed for years
the ball disappears. Among the chickasaw

plums. Among the swaggering
pipit who wag their tails and sing

Oh, winter is gone. In every nook
and cranny you look winter has gone.
Taking those howls from the walls.

Those mice, those nails from the rafters
clicking, clicking. That ice.
All that cold in the bones is gone.

And walking now like anyone,
even like philosophers,

they are lost, lost
in a dreamy geometry. Looking for their ball!

Full of summer! Full of an afternoon
that will not come again. Following one

behind the other. A little pageant hip-deep
in timothy. In sweet plum. In burrs
and something they cannot name.

And have no wish to name.

One Bright Autumn

One bright autumn up on a scaffold
my Uncle Russ began dancing—
a story and a half off the ground
he shimmied and shook like no one
I knew, like someone possessed,
until my father knocked him down.
He knocked him down to my feet
swinging a two-by-four like a bat.

My uncle sat and looked empty,
like a man who'd been caught
in pure delight, by passion,
and after a wild ride tossed aside.
Why'd you grab that live wire, Russ?
My uncle rubbed his head: he said
he was dreaming and lost his balance,
he said he felt like a fool.

Forty years later beside the swollen
Clearwater I toss my insignificant stone.
It seemed so easy. One dreamy day
my foolish uncle, lost in something
he himself could not explain,
reached out and grabbed a river rushing by.
My lucky father, knowing what to do,
simply brought him back.

On Certain Cold Days

On certain cold days
I wear a wool shirt
that belonged to my father.
I also have his hammer
and the last pencil he used—
the one tool we had in common.

At a museum once, at a time
when doctors were keeping close
tabs on his heart, keeping him
off the job and miserable,
I asked what did he think?
He said if I was buying
he'd rather be on a scaffold.

I have his blue eyes,
a lot of his impatience
to make things fit,
but could I tie my aching
molar to a gut leader,
the leader to my hammer,
and swing?

I watched this, shocked,
and then he grinned.
A dentist would have taken longer,
gummed up his whole day,

and made him pay besides.
Look: wide awake,
right back to work,
and nothing hurt.

My Polish Grandfather

> We live, as we dream—alone.
> —*Heart of Darkness*

Before he began to disappear
he'd take his thumping Belgians, Nelly and Prince,
down to the creek for a drink
and go in with them, boots and all,
and lay his burnt face on the water, his mustache
spreading out like fine muzzle hairs,
and rise up shaking. Or dropping

his pitchfork among the cowpies
he'd weave away to the orchard, and for hours
sit there in the high timothy
gazing at the sky—
I'd climb a limb and watch
and wonder what held him so still, and what
the fire was like that had left him

those sleek, pink patches across his cheek.
My mother's angry explanation that he
came from the Old Country packed
in a boat with only a loaf of bread
and the clothes on his back
and made rich men richer breaking his back
made no sense to me. Once

when the black bull tore loose
and came and lowered his head

breathing hard into Grandma's chicken yard,
and we looked at each other, he burst
from the barn, the pink patches bright as rhubarb,
and grabbing the chain linked to the bull's nose
he pulled and jerked more furious

than I had ever seen him,
until I thought he would rip
it out, until their dark foreheads
were touching, pressing into each other, both of them
moaning like two fighters
who have had enough
but still can't quit

—and then on his knees he was embracing
that big black head and whispering
as if he held a baby.
We never spoke—
all the summers I followed him around,
not one word to each other.
But once—once!—he picked me up and sat me

on the hay wagon between his knees,
and gave me the reins to hold,
and clicked his tongue to move Prince and Nelly along—
along faster! Calling *Gee!* and *Haw!*
until Grandma came rushing out,
her fist, her skirts,
and the Polish flying—

and he, his hands over mine,
helped me steer the wagon
around and around her, and all the while a fine gold shower
of haydust falling, and he crooning those sounds I can still hear
when I am happy.
Nights after chores,
the kerosene lamp's honeyed glow

softening his scars, he began to disappear.
He did this so quietly and smoothly I could not believe
he would return in the morning.
Night after night in that honeyed light
he ate his soup and bread, he knelt
on the floor hunched over his rosary
like a small bear come from the woods,

from farther and farther away in his throat
came the sound, the murmur of a man
raising a glass of whiskey to his lips, the same
sound I hear in my own throat now,
and then from inside his shirt,
where at first I thought he himself would crawl,
he brought forth a book and was gone.

The summer I stayed in the city to start baseball
Grandma found him beside the hollyhocks.
On my eleventh birthday, in a satin box,
he lay with pennies on his eyes, his trimmed mustache

become an almost perfect caterpillar,
his pink patches, his face
white and shiny as a bowl. Hot

all over, I slipped away to the creek
and took off my blue wool suit, and drank, and shook
my head like a horse, and saw falling on the water
nothing more than my skinny shadow.
But years later Grandma, very old, said oh yes
there were so many things to remember, that awful day
on the wagon, and when the bull got out, and how peaceful

he looked beside the hollyhocks all in bloom
holding that Korzeniowski again, that Pole
he was always so quiet with—but why?
She did not understand why.
Taking her ruby hands, trembling to explain,
I said Grandma please
may I see that last book he was holding?

And she gazed at the door
as if he might come in now from chores
and sit with us, looking girlish, lost,
was somewhere else when she finally told me no, I couldn't.
Just before Mr. Savage, the undertaker, closed the coffin—
you remember him, he was such a nice man—
she put it there where he could find it.

The Wolverine

Word got around town: a wolverine was being shown in Rae Brothers parking lot. Some last-minute Christmas shoppers went to look. Many of the younger people had never seen one before, not up close like this. It lay curled in the back of a pickup, on the tailgate, and someone—a small girl—said it looked like a big fuzzy caterpillar. The man holding her hand said, "See those teeth? You wouldn't want to fool with them!" And somebody else asked, "What is it?" The ranger, who had received it from the trapper, said it was a male. About thirty pounds. He said he was surprised: wolverines were supposed to have been long gone from the area. The trapper was surprised too: he'd been after bobcat. He had his foot up on a rear tire and was leaning against his knee; his hat was pushed back; he could look down and see the animal as he talked. The man holding the small girl's hand asked what he used to catch it. "A snare," the other said. "With that good aircraft cable that don't kink." He shook his head at the surprise of it all, or at the snare's effectiveness, or maybe only as a kind of punctuation; and a couple of older men, whose eyes were watery-bright from age, shook their heads too. It got cold standing there in Rae Brothers parking lot, and people began drifting away. One of these, a girl, said to her boyfriend, "I hate those things." He laughed, then flung his arm around her neck, pulling her closer.

A Late Detail from the Depression

"One freezing day," my mother began, "I'm looking around at all the cold—the apartment, the building, the whole world's an iceberg—and guess what? I'm wrong. We're on fire." Well, I knew this story—I had grown up with it. I lay in my crib, on the third floor, and my frantic young mother wrapped me quickly in her ratty muskrat coat and ran down through smoke and flames licking the walls, and didn't stop until she reached Frei Dieboldt's Garage two blocks away. Where she burst through a door wailing my father's name. I knew all this and in my mind raced ahead to finish the story for her—which of course had a happy ending. But once inside the garage, she suddenly added a fresh detail. After all these years! There, at that exact moment, she said, was my father holding up the rear end of a Pontiac coupe that had slipped off the jack so Frei's other mechanic, who was underneath, could breathe. "This is true," she said, "don't look at me like a goof." Well, it might have been a less fancy kind of car, she admitted, what difference did it make? They lost everything, all their wedding gifts, clothes, thirty dollars she had saved in a jelly jar, what would they do! "But *you*," she said, "you were howling your head off because your pants were full, which you hated, and were hungry, mad too I was holding you so tight, and I was bawling like crazy myself, sobbing, *Ted! Ted!* And he just stood there blue in the face, that sweet man, couldn't talk, couldn't move, or that poor unlucky devil squirming on the greasy floor—you could only see his legs—would've got more than some ribs busted, and I didn't understand any of it. . . ." She took a deep breath. I waited for the happy ending, which had to do with hugging and thanking their lucky stars. But gazing off at the sun going down, sending out long red wings across the horizon, my mother only sighed, "Look at that, would you?" Then resumed raking her leaves as if no one were around.

Close to Trees

He was only a boy and hard
on his heart lay a terrible fear—
that any minute he might slip away
like smoke or a dream
and be no more, be gone forever,
if he didn't stay close to trees.
So every day on his way up the street
he'd pull up a plant that looked
like a tree—something he could hold—
and carry it over his heart to school,
keeping all of him from harm.
Here comes Paul! the children called,
and called out louder, beginning to dance
and squeal, as day by day the plants
he brought grew larger and larger,
in fact became seedlings and saplings—
maple and birch and evergreen.
Pulled up with such brute, confusing need
(some even thought the need evil)
that everyone, alarmed, stepped back.
Clearly the boy was ill,
who couldn't see it?
Everyone saw it. The doctors—
and over the years there were many
(and many tears)—finally got Paul
to let the trees be where they were
and just carry some leaves in his pocket.

And then—a great victory—just one leaf,
like a rabbit's foot, or a bullet
that had come very close,
or a picture of someone dear,
which he kept in an envelope.

Part Two

A Dream in the Carpathians

After I died I began to wonder
where my grave would be. On a hill
among shady trees? Near a golden river?
In the center, oh God, of a buzzing cloverleaf?
An old friend I hadn't seen in years came dancing by
wearing a bow tie and a stovepipe hat, and said, "It's bad,
not having any home—I know—but what I've done
is leave a note, with arrows pointing out the way,
funny directions to make everyone laugh."
We laughed at the brilliance of this notion
and then, doffing his hat, he was off, oddly dodging
the monuments and stones crowding around us,
as if playing a kind of cops-and-robbers.
I woke. The room was lit with sky, with fall, and a coppery
light from at least three countries—
and the warm girl smiling beside me
whom I loved, had loved last night in the mountain's
glow, said, "Well, here we are on Baba, did you sleep okay?"
I told about my friend, his brilliant plan, his hat,
and how he scampered off, apparently in a cemetery.
"How strange," she said, looking sadly away,
"I dreamt you were dying, I think in a theatre—
I was crying, sick with grief, and yet I wanted,
terribly, to fuck you one more time. I even
used that word, I didn't care who heard me.
Oh, but it was all right, you whispered kindly,
like an old doctor, both arms reaching up

to help me down, considerate of my dress, my hair,
and saying—they were your last words—
you had a long, important speech to make and would be
practicing now. That was the hard part, darling—
your being so nice about it, so polite."

The Bunker in the Parsley Fields

Among the common folk and their uncommonly tasty tomatoes,
among the mothers of beautiful babies, the leggy, oiled Misses
coiling for crowns on TV weekly, and the coiffed
bodyguards watching the crowds watching the President tool into town
and bow and receive yet another bouquet of flowers,
among the billowing, bountiful smoke hazing the hills
and good firm cabbage heads almost everywhere,
    the word is:
the best capitalists, hands down, are former communists
—especially if they had a finger on some socialist
loot, a key to the strongbox, a secret
Swiss number to get them jumping, look
at their nice big fenced-in houses going up, no
smothering prefab flats for these operators, no muck
under their nails, no unfinished bunkers shooting out rats, sprouting
rust-furry twisted rods of steel, like shocked eels, in their
    front yards, no Parsley Fields.
I am in the Parsley Fields, six floors up
watching this boy straight down bang his trike
over and over: he rolls back, waits a moment gathering
steam, then head lowered, a little bull, pedals hard
smack into the bunker again. It doesn't budge, of course, it
sits there more solid than Papa, the size
of a soccer field, roofless, as high above ground
as the boy is tall, walls so thick he can
lie across them anywhere and not hang over, deep
as two or three placid elephants standing one

on top the other, making no sound, no raised trumpet calls,
no crap, what would the boy think of a trick like that?
     This bunker, these
stacked-up flats where thousands cook and stew
and see inside the box another queen take home a perfect ermine
fur, an airline ticket, stuff to cream, color, butter, and dust
herself all over, stretch for miles along the Danube—
into a repetition that shimmers at the ends
as heat shimmers on the summer highway just ahead
and makes your eyes water if you look too long. And it's
called the Parsley Fields, this place, not because in the Greek root
parsley means rock and stone, but because
once upon a time some people can still remember
that delicate herb declared itself abundantly on these banks,
where in the early hours our tenor neighbor upstairs
will wake us calling softly for Carmen
and finish off by screaming nothing not even wretched
Don José would understand, as if an old poem
he had written on coarse paper, or a rope,
got stuck in his throat,
where the moon spreads out
at the bottom of a hard, wet notion
that now official change has come
no one knows what to do with except this boy
who rams and rams it wearing
three little ruts in the mud.

Picked Out a Toka, a Stanley

picked out a Jonathan and Gala one morning
from Alice Rickman soothing her Manx. Old cat possessed
fresh bumps, a boxer's pushed-in aspect, and tender
need. Looks Irish, looks like my friend Red,
I said, taking a break from throwing his kid
batting practice on the Nebraska prairie.
Under a Greek fisherman's cap, two scuffed knees
showing through her bibs, Alice said No Problem's
what we call it. Said what a day. Smiled. Everywhere
you looked she had things breathing, lifting up,
flicking out little jabs and nods at the sun.
Fine, filigreed wings of water, *wish* and then *wish*,
issued over her shoulder. Remember, she said, trees appreciate
some freedom, above all they favor a nice mucky soup
to start out from. Gave Lizzie No Problem to hold
and me a hand lifting the trees in my rig. Drove
up the mountain past Fred's MULE CROSSING
sign, past Bailey's grazing mares, past the black-
berry patch bears were leaving their big seeded
cigar rolls in. Up and up. Hauling an orchard
for the kid Lizzie and I started six months
back in Slovakia, in a boxy prefab Socialist high-rise
complete with a crumbling bunker, the principal view
beyond our window cement, me fifty-four, a grand-
father, Lizzie thirty-eight. Hold on, she said,
slow down and tell how we strolled beside the Danube,
all those kings looking stiff on their stone thrones,

how I said get ready for a big surprise.
You said it, I said, and continued digging my three holes
in the rocky slope our cat, Oshkosh, plucks mice from,
plus one under the window the kid can lean out
and breathe in wafts of blossoming, hear the honeyed
buzz of sweet dustings, the juicy enterprise. All day
I dug, separating rock and old root and some antlered bone
from their deep suck. Two apple, two plum.
That's four bases, I said, a home run. Tell how
Alice said deer, come snow, will covet your tender bark,
that's a good line, it fits you, Lizzie said. Not right
now, right now, I said, I want to get philosophical.
I want to get my bat and knock a rock
for luck into the valley, into the long view
the kid will have tasting this ontological fruit.
I want to dig in and knock it
all the way back to that river ancient tribes are still
squabbling over, where I stood holding a bag
of apples and plums and knew, as you know only a precious few
things in this mapped-over, flowing life
what your big surprise was.
Did you really know? she said. Tell the truth.
I had to, I said, what could be bigger or sweeter?

The Sister

for Gretchen

In the earth-breath of my barn,
in the wood shed where I split and stack
years of flicker knocks and owl hoots,
out in the piney air my corral keeps fresh,
I cannot stop my arms from flapping—
like a cock pheasant all feathered up

I'm about to fly yonder across the valley
to Blacktail Ridge, give that old buck goat
watching me something to see,
a man with a new daughter, a father
whose first-born came to assist at her sister's birth,
stroking the mother-pain, embracing, bringing back

how her hands fluttered to my cheeks when I bent close,
how she fell from pure abandonment dancing in the grass
to clutching my chest while the doctor sewed up her slashed foot,
how twenty-eight years slipped by, her flight
into photos and notes, calls in the night sometimes thousands
of miles from where each of us felt the spinning,

returned now as this random, late snowflake
comes down the mountain and catches my wrist,
allowing me a moment to hold and praise
no matter where I turn or how hard I wave,
going sweetly mad at its intricate joinery,
its own sweet praise and departure.

Dogtoothed Violets

I don't know how a dog's mouth
got involved in their naming.
I know I can eat them
if I don't eat too many,
and come April when the snow is slipping
in rivulets down my mountain
I know bear and deer will pause and enjoy them
as I enjoy a truly fresh salad smelling of meadow and shaded wood,—
and I know in some ways we are all like dogs,
or ought to be, in matters like faithfulness and sleep
and nursing our young.
But these delicate gold-colored wonders are much closer,
as I see it, to a piano off in the wings
bringing our daughters out in their toe shoes,
that first bright performance at which we beam and beam
until our hearts burst into flame.
A tiny flame, yes? And lasting
for only such a short time—
the time it takes to compose ourselves,
if we can, if we are that lucky.

In the Garden with Margaret

On the little hill groomed and stocked with seed
we show ourselves, one long shadow
in the sun now fully pushed
above Blacktail Ridge across the valley.
Fresh from sleep we have come to see
the dewy young, a sudden flicker, the bee who feathers
our strawberry plants like an idea so good
how can it settle down to simple business?
And here is Mr. Hat, the ski-pole-and-coat-hanger
scarecrow I devised, to remind the deer
that some among us will open our arms all night
in the right kind of light, and even smell
—and I am happy to see her laugh when I lift
the damp shirt to my nose to recognize myself. Ah yes,
I fancy she is saying, you and the showy cabbage
have survived to another day! Of course
she has no words yet.
But when I fall on my knees
to the newest green shoots coming through,
whispering, So, this is the world—
she will look and look, almost not breathing,
and then move, like the most subtle of conductors,
her tiny fingers.

The Cougar

The cougar who prowls my mountain came down
close today and looked at me in my corral
—we looked at each other. A fine mist
lay among the wild oats growing there and there
he stood, not moving. I was on my knees.

Over his shoulder I could see Gospel Hump
an hour away, still covered with snow.
It was quiet and raining lightly and my hands
which had been cold from pulling up
thistles, were now warm.

For a moment I wanted nothing more
than to lie in the snow on Gospel Hump and slowly
move my arms, making a great angel.
Then I wanted my father to be alive again
and see this magnificence with me—
we wouldn't have to say anything,
I just wanted to hold his hand.

Everything was very clear—the pointy buds
on my plum trees nearby, his eyes, the dark whorls
the knots made in the boards of my fence.
I wanted to see him shake his head in wonder.
Just once. The way he did after finishing a tough job,
or when he had to admit he was happy.

I don't know how long the cougar stayed,
but I was glad to see him turn and go back—
he went back as smoothly it seemed as a trout
in water—and I returned to my thistles,
whose almost silky white root slips out
so easily when it rains.

Flicker

After I lit the sticks and closed
the door to my wood stove,
I heard a commotion inside
sounding like leaves pushed around
by wind, sounding like the crisp
and trembling reds and yellows
of fall outside, the mountain, my high
retreat—recalling the dead
maple I had cut earning
my dinner and book, my doze
into an evening of comfort.
Then it came again, the rustle
turned to a scratching, a cry, thin
and lost, the sigh of a long
weariness the bearer did not wish
to inflict on anyone and yet
what can we do sometimes? I flung
the door open and saw, back
to a wall of furry soot, a large
bird in bird outrage, a flicker,
giving me a small black eye,
a furious, go-away, see-
what-you've-done-this-time eye. I
looked at it—a female—amazed
that she wanted me (and surely
that eye wanted me) to leave her alone.
I saw smoke shrouding her
proud, beautiful crown and thrust in

my hand. Scattering soot, dust, chips
of char, she flew to the stove's deepest
reach, would rather cook
than let me help. I closed off
the damper, shut the door.
I cursed the pipe her messing around
brought her down, the smoke building up, her
skittishness. And after yelling St. Paul's bitter
advice (better to marry than burn!)
I cursed my wit. And my hand
for not being quicker.
                    Now if I opened
the flue to give her air, air
would feed the fire. If I opened the door
giving her room to see the light
I could see my house filling with smoke
—we'd both choke, her frantic flight
throwing sparks everywhere, my cedar
and pine retreat flaring. I felt
stuck, foot-tied to that spot, not even
able to run for a bucket of water.
So I decided (I guess I decided) to hope
she would faint in there, then
I could haul her out. Thus I became a man
waiting for a voice in the deep
cave of his making to stop
saying *oh* and *ah*. And it would not.
And wanting to hurl my own outrage

at that pecker into the small
and wormy, that nuisance, that independence, that
fear, I opened the flue, the door, opened
everything I could run to
and out she came in a glide
air and wings and outstretched
unfaithful arms are made for, rising,
crashing into her shadow, into her likeness
flashed on the glass protecting a prize
picture of the Grand Canyon, into
at last her glory,
leaving behind only a fine
salmon-colored rump feather
in my ash.

The Great Horned Owl

also called *cat owl*
—*Webster's*

Ever since our cat Oshkosh disappeared
a great horned owl, *Bubo virginianus*,
has been slamming into the house.
I say that as if it's a common occurrence,
but twice last month and again today
seems a lot—especially when we're eating lunch
and suddenly there she is, beautifully spread out
about a dozen feet from the window, swooping down
like God's craziest angel . . .
                              We're grateful
and relieved, after the bang and fall,
she's able to fly—
none too gracefully—but away she goes
to a big red fir at the edge of our yard
and settles her head, the finely barred pedestal
of feathers holding it up, the famous eyes turned
slitty, Oriental,
as if nothing really has happened, my friends,
and now it's time for a nap.

For as long as she sits there,
my wife will move nowhere
she can't see the tree, and not whisper
exactly but quietly turn off the radio
if it is playing, and pick up Margaret

just in case she might suddenly cry out.
And we wait. All three of us watching
in a kind of belief I can't mock,
my wife pressing her cheek
to the baby's, saying, "See, honey?"
and after a while, almost wistfully,
"Well, we had fish again, didn't we?"
and then today when the owl finally leaped away
down the valley, seeming on purpose to barely miss
crashing into several aspen embracing autumn,
"Oh! how she always needs to show off."

Lavina

I'd been looking over the slick sag of clay
slope below my corral, thinking about erosion,
what I could plant in that sorry soil
that would take, and there, a short toss away
ran a nuthatch—clicking its tiny claws on a larch—
and after a moment, ecstatic, Lavina.
When I blinked the image was gone.
I had to sit down. Alive she was strictly applied
science, nothing touched her that wouldn't
be put to some practical use, and the one time
I saw her cry it was quick, a sneeze-like
little shock, and I wanted to hide. Lavina—
Vi—was a woman in loud sensible shoes constantly
turning and finding something across the room
that should have been somewhere else, or polished,
or, like the perfect wax pear I once left imperfect
marks of my hunger in, removed. For years I thought
she was built mostly along the lines of a stork's
bones I'd seen in a book, and I couldn't guess how
round Gramps, devoted to the slow-growing ash
of his stogy—and long naps in the piney woods—
kept up with her. (To get the hot garlicky sausage
she would not allow near the house, he brought it to us.)
She lived to be almost ninety and spent the last
thirty years—without Gramps—keeping close tabs
on her money, her sons, and her mileage,
or so the family summary went. My father,

her first-born, she left alone (because of my mother)
but Karl and Ralph—and the sheriff too—she rode,
as they put it, unmercifully, for merely thinking aloud
she consider hiring a driver.
I could still see her swiping a Kleenex
over the Hudson's gleaming dash, her lips fixed
in forward, my uncles—who worked with their hands,
who made her lumberyard hum—unable to lift a finger
until she roared away. Then maybe
they'd kick at something. (Once I saw Karl break up his ruler.)
My grandmother's favorite story, to which she kept time
by banging her cane, was how, first, Tolfree, the so-called banker,
ran off with half of their savings, and wrecked Gramps'
ticker—forget the doctor's baloney—
followed by pork chop lawyers—three in a row!—
who stole from her blind. One even went to St. Joe's
and played rummy with Father Rau, so don't go
bellowing trust, when Homer changed her oil
she made him hold up the stick.
Thus my grandmother, for years shifting her own gears, purled
among laggards and thieves and dust, and cut every speck
of fat from her meat. And cried once
that I know of, seeing my father's casket.
But she recovered fast, and furiously
polished her glasses—exactly as she did
when Gramps, on his deathbed, reached over
whether in delirium or on purpose
and held my mother's hand. Like the elephant,

people said, Vi never forgot a thing,
and indeed on every grand- and great-grand-
child's birthday she wrote out a check.
No foolish card with balloons
or candles you'd throw away anyway,
no message of any kind
beyond the money she must have figured
everyone would understand, or learn
by and by to be wary of. In a hand
small and squiggly as tree moss or nuthatch tracks
or the crazy patterns in clay after it rains.

Collecting Cowpies

In sweet soggy spring
when the mountain is soft
and we file down the road
past lilac, plum
and the bowing dog-
toothed violet,
one behind the other
following our wheelbarrow,
it is to ease ourselves
onto Fred's pasture.
We go Lizzie through first,
then Margaret who grips
an old serving spoon
as I hand her over
the three strands of wire,
then me with my shovel.
We have come to collect
Fred's wonderful cowpies.
We are veterans at this   .
simple maneuver of
scooping up
perfect brown plops
turned crusty on top
in the feathery green,
and dropping them in
boxes stamped George
Dickel, Celestial Orange
Tea, and Western Family

Grade A Honey.
We can't wipe off
a goofy grin, feeling lucky,
feeling connected to the genius
who or which keeps
turning everything over—
and we can think of nothing
we'd rather be doing right
now, under a pale halo
of moon floating round the valley
and giddily holding on
to our mountain,
than taking this gift,
these rich ruminations,
back up the road
one behind the other
following our wheelbarrow.

The Stone

On the rocky slope
below my orchard
I found a tremendous stone—
with what seemed a perfect
red moon, or the sun,
locked inside it.
I couldn't lift this prize
but I could push it. A little.
And a little more—
and after a time
my wife came out
and looking down she called:
What on earth, are you crazy!
I couldn't explain—
the stone and I had got
to a place at which
explanation would cost us,
a place very close to
balance for a moment.
I could barely say help me.
But she saw how it was
and scrambled down, in the
wrong shoes, no gloves,
and together we shoved.
We shoved and paused
all afternoon, lost
between the slope

and our shoulders—
and once in the easier-going
orchard, in laughter.
But we kept on, maybe even
pushing harder.
The sun went down,
the moon slipped out,
and in that white glow
we stopped.
We had to.
The great stone
against the house
and under the window
where we slept
could go no farther.

Delicately in Small Measure

On clear nights, drifting off,
I sometimes tuck away stars
I am told are no longer there
though I see them. For years
I have done this—
as a little game, I suppose,
against death. I have saved
as well those kisses the sweet-natured
calico gave to my daughter,
delicately in small measure,
before owl took her away,
and the bounding hound-mix
Hondo's big splashy *los besos*
I save as a matter of course,
and the pure quiet of her
looking upon deer looking, their gazes
locked in long astonishment.
Drifting off I vote for
long astonishment, and the rare
showing of cougar above the corral,
the ropy music of its tail
going up and down
and her following it,
as she will follow hawk
going round and round
with the sun, its shadow
brushing her upturned cheek,

and geese in elegant long-necked stretch
honking and honking,
and a dizzy leaf descending,
and a pine cone squirrel
has finished chewing on,
all such earthy pearls
which she must hold
samples of in both hands
perhaps forever—
first in front of her,
then behind—
though in a moment
when I bend down close
to see her prizes,
eagerly she gives them up, glowing,
as if this is what we do.

A Lullaby

Sleep, my daughter, sleep,
and when you wake
to everything that's quick
and breathes in every part of you,
dream, my daughter, dream.

Part Three

Prayer

O compost heap
taker of what we can't eat
keeper of pucker and soak

receive this peel
this sapless berry cane
embrace these old maids

rolled up at the bottom
of the popcorn bowl

the cob the mob of silk
the curlicued leaf
and papery husk

O let the blackest part
of my horse manure pile
become as honey

the dewy root
round which we dance

caught in a happy confusion
among stem and flower
sheets and tiny socks

worms bees rain
a sky
the color of apricots

In St. Peter's Home for Nuns

In St. Peter's Home for Nuns
there is only one remaining,
ancient, bent, bifocaled
Sister Ambrozine—
who spends her day in full black habit
giving half to Him and half to
Gaius Julius Caesar
and his histories.
For lunch, in Gaul,
she takes a little cheese.
The diocese would like to
close this place—utilities alone,
the bishop's secretary sighs,
are killing, plus
the attic's rife with birds,
God save us.
But he knows the woman
and what's worse,
she knows him—
they go back to high school
when she taught him Latin.
Never once did Sister
need to twist good Father's
ear to hear the music.
In third, for God's sake, person
is how she makes him
drive out twice on weekends—
Saturday to hear her trifling sins,

Sunday to say Mass—
when at least three other priests
are more convenient!
No. And no, she won't be moved
until he buries her.
If she were merely mad, a harridan . . .
At confession: through that crack
between her teeth stylish Caesar
still emerges whistling.
And Sundays after celebrating
Christ's great sacrifice,
that's chocolate from a sack
of Hershey's Kisses on her lips.

Skookumchuck

We came to Skookumchuck and quickly
slipped our shoes and socks off, first
the baby's. No one else was there. I rolled
my pants up, joined the cold rushing Salmon
at the edge, its careless humming, rainbows
nosing close, darting, pebbles plump
and bright as mushrooms on the bottom.
The baby, reaching, wanted in. I took her hands—
I held her up and slowly let her down, up and down,
her tiny feet and mine together in a row. She squealed
to see hers big, then small, then smaller. On the beach
her mother crawled in circles, clawing up
a castle: digging fingers down, pulling darker
sand to shape this heap. "Maybe I am
dreaming after all," she said. "Hold me, hold me."
She didn't mean for me or anyone to hold her,
and yet I saw her going off, lost inside
the dream, gathering together sand, river,
harsh, brilliant sun spots everywhere downstream—
all of us. There we went, that fast—
and up on Haystack Mountain a solitary
cow or bull, a black shadow like a dumb
unmoving cloud to whom we all meant
nothing, watching. I could yell or pray
or not and there we went because
the rushing, humming Salmon took us. "Oh no,"
she sang, "oh no you don't," and holding the baby
I saw she only meant that something small
had fallen in her moat, a ladybug or something
valuable that needed saving, and she would save it.

Umbels

In my dream I had the names reversed:
I had Sweet Cicely the horse,
Lucille flowering from her mane.
She bowed just low enough to blow
moist breath across my cheek.
I woke, sat up, could hear Lucille whinny
sharp, impatient, in the valley.
I eased myself outside: stars and moon
looked normal, from a tree, way up,
a pine cone fell—*pwak, pwak*—
a noise like branches breaking into flame.
The grass was wet, the stones
I stepped on hurt. It seemed important
I achieve the garden fast, as if for safety,
but I wasn't frightened—cold a little,
wished I had a shirt on, shoes.
Then I saw my daughter's sandbox:
right away I covered up
my feet, my legs. I was perfectly
aware of every stupid move—
plus her cups and spoons, a baseball cap
damp with dew. I tried it on, too small.
Slowly I lay back and did the rest:
my chest, the other arm and hand. Okay,
where's Lucille? "You've got to hold," she said,
"your hand out flat when offering an apple."
She demonstrated how, this city kid,
a skinny pup, dying. They

bring them out to love an animal.
"That's Sweet Cicely I put around her,
several umbels of it." Twelve or so. Almost
no color, no hair. You forget their names.

I Call My Mother

"Hi," I say, "how's it going?" "Hi," she says, "not good. Everything is breaking down—the mixer, waffle iron, my *toaster* which I got when you were six! What next? Last week that, this week this. They don't make one thing like they used to. Now it's eight o'clock and people who know something, or think they do, are out, cutting a rug, having their laughs. Me? My kitchen's full of steam! Beets and steam! Why? Because I'm canning, that's why. All these lovely beets Rita gave me, oh you never tasted anything so sweet, I can't let them go to *waste*. By the way, did you hear? Eddie Hill is dead." Eddie Hill? Dead? "Well, I guess you wouldn't know, living way out there. Almost two weeks ago. Heart attack the paper said. Fifty-six, that's your age. . . ." Eddie's boyish face, his big sunny smile after snapping off a perfect roundhouse curve comes up. He taught me how to throw it, how to drop-kick, pole-vault, scale a perch with beer caps. Dead? His father had a rabbit, Buck, that almost knocked the hutch apart when Eddie put a doe in. All those years I hadn't seen my friend. Why? Because I couldn't stand to hang around and lose the motion he had helped me start? My mother's saying, ". . . no, no, I have work to do, before the whole damn house comes down! Oh, he says, and stands there like a dope, every hair in place, giving me this long, lost-dog look he's so *adept* at. I thought we had a date, he says. You know, he's younger than me, only seventy-six, but what a baby. Go, I tell him, go show your duds and fancy la-de-dahs to somebody else, go on, get out of here. So I sent the bum away. And stay away! I said. Oh, he'll be back. When I'm good and ready I can dance till dawn, *all* the dances, and he knows it."

Josef of Moravia

The last time I saw Josef he was walking away like a man wearing only a single shoe and not doing much to stay level. When he stopped, turning to wave one last time, both hands held out, he looked for a moment like a scarecrow in a field—an unlikely, portly, red-bearded scarecrow. But what could Josef frighten away, really? Birds? Deer? Mangy, ill-mannered dogs? He would welcome them! He would welcome anything or anyone free. Even Gypsies. Even the Gypsies he told me about who burst one time into his sleeper on the night train from Prague and tried to help him appreciate, deeply, the fiddle and their foul Soviet tobacco, the odors of ancient river camps and raw onions and Bulgarian wine, the layers of ripe rags they took off as their songs and the little compartment heated up. "But I could not appreciate their—how do you call it?—their importunate gas, I'm afraid. I have several Ph.D.s in that subject from hearing and hearing my betters during the recent long stink."

Smiling, he held both arms up higher. I waved back. Goodbye, gentle, fierce old scholar! Then he continued aiming, more or less, toward the library, where he would begin by opening a window—and a boy came to me, a boy who does what boys do, getting dirty, drawing unlikely, sprawling pictures, riding no-hands on a bicycle, and having all the usual worries, but none about staying clean or staying in line or even of falling over.

Sunday Morning: Marilee Combs Her Red Hair

"Speaking of time, love,
and the human grip, my
Alabama grandmother would
sit me down and say,
'Marilee, honey, did I ever
tell you about my mishap?'
'Yes, Grandma, you have.'
'Well, there was this man
with a wooden leg—
and it went clear up
from his shoes to where
a person like your turnip-
hearted daddy will jiggle loose
change in his pocket. . . .'
She worked Daddy in here
real fast because after
that mishap he undid the starter
button on her Fiesta.
Even so, she'd fix her a
pretty bonnet on tight and go
sit behind the wheel, her teeth
in her lap, making fierce
sputtering noises.
I never saw this part
but sometimes Daddy would
lean his elbow

in the window and say,
'Mama, aren't you kickin
this poor old horse a
little hard?' She'd flip
the radio on and drown
him out with Elvis or
Dolly Parton or some
preacher hollering hey you
send me a five-dollar
love gift sister
and I'll send you a plastic
tablecloth with Jesus
Day-Gloed in the middle.
You would like my Daddy.
His name is Henry Clay
but Grandma till she quit
this vale called him Rodney."

2

"What would you do if
you were a nifty prince
turned into a fly
—like that one there
in the window—
and you were banging your
nose on the glass, trying to

get away because a maid, ugly
as worms in General Sherman's
grin, aimed to smack you
all over heaven?
And to make matters worse
this is the well-preserved
Queen's personal bedroom
we're talking about,
and you really wanted to stay
and play in her fruit bowl,
sniff around the royal ruff,
and hope when she woke up
she'd say the magic word
—which is a common everyday
word she'd be ready any
second to utter—
and set you fully free
from awful, sticky fly-ness,
back into your lean
and burning state of skin-
over-milk-white-bone.
Would you keep banging away
to escape that hairy, midriff-
spongy hireling who hated
your insides, or would you
flex up, baby,
and hold out for the prize?"

3

"Well, what happened was,
Grandma, who was way over
in the far right-hand lane,
pulled a sure sudden
left-hand maneuver,
shocking I can imagine
the other two lanes of same-
way traffic high-tailing it
west to Mississippi,
and sideswiped the man
wearing his wooden leg.
It was a pretty day,
she recalled. You could smell
all kinds of piney-laced
whiff and even hear,
she declared, the delicate
cooing of a dove. So
she and the gentleman
engaged in real nice
conversation for a while.
He had gone to Tuscaloosa
before the war, to read
history, and yes ma'am
he knew from both books
and real life that just
lifting your head off

a soft pillow at sunrise
was taking a chance, that
order and chaos were tough
customers, you bet, requiring
a careful eye on them, but
when you spilt milk or mussed
a paint job, wasn't that pretty
much where reflection came in?
So right there beside a buzzing
cloverleaf they reflected on how
lucky they'd been to meet,
and to've had a chance,
in this crazy world bent on
whizzing after Lord knew
what, to discuss ideas.
The main one being cooperation
of course and its golden glow. . . .
Baby, be an angel and scratch
my back? Right over where
Oklahoma eases by Arkansas?
Oh, that's good. . . .
I can see a great big Brahma
bull nosing up juicy tufts
of milo . . . and a quick
little miss in a sundress
skipping past it on the sly.
I believe she is feeling
the first itches of

girlhood. Lord, a whole bunch
of red curls is unfurling
in her wake. No doubt young
Billy Bob will soon be all
afroth and breathing something
wicked down her freckled neck.
Damn. Now I'm hungry.
Where can we find us a bowl
of grits with lots of
cinnamon sprinkled on top?
But hold on, don't stop
that generous business
under my kidneys, sugar.
I am moving into this
new chapter not real fast,
and you are doing exactly
the right thing, like a knight
of times gone by. . . ."

In Puerto Rico, She Says

when boy meets girl
and so on, first
they are *amiguitos*
which means for example
a nice little walk, nothing
enormous, maybe a stop for
coconut at a *bohío*
to fix up their thirst. Okay.

More walking. No big
deal. Very easy.
But soon they discover
they really can talk
and are sad
not to be closer, yes?
Maybe all week
surrounded by school

she is thinking, Oh I can't
wait till Friday
I am away from all that!
For him
this also is true.
He tries smoking. Hey!
he spits,
what a dull activity,

it's not in my character!
So they become *novios*
which means nobody else
and the parents of each,
nothing enormous, meet.
Over plantains,
shrimps, it's very polite
and so on, and sometimes,

not always,
the couple they get *precomprometidos*
which means pre-
engaged and she
wears a very, very
small,
very tiny
ring, okay maybe

a token only
that she will like to hold
by her nice underthings
could be,
or by mementos
from her sweet grand-mama,
in a drawer. So
they have been several months, oh

such a long time
walking like this. But notice
a very large thing!
They really *really* enjoy it
and want to be
always hugging and so on.
They are still
novios but now they are also

están comprometidos!
which means exactly the same
only more.
Let me hear you
say it. Yes, good, but
you must practice rolling
over your tongue a little bit
the r's. For this part

of course everyone comes,
uncles, aunts,
they dance and eat
and like *that*
happens along the event
you are waiting for!
No, no,
in Puerto Rico

east, west, north, and south
mean nothing—
only left, right,
up, and down.
If you are lost
drive fifteen minutes
then stop and ask.
It's like that for example.
Very easy.

Dear Friends

Though it is true
that if our nose itches
in a certain way
we will kiss a fool—
and equally so
that if the fool turns
into a toad
and pees in our hand,
it is too bad.
But consider the riches
of waters everywhere,
and all their relations,
as does good father heron
from his vestry of sticks,
on his lonely leg,
keeping that vigil
for which we pay nothing:
the devilish fire
in the turtle's eye,
the duck he covets,
the cloud of fry,
and all blown wildflowers,
all soupy weeds,
and especially their showy parts
where the seeds are
(that scatter
and gather on their own
owing nothing to those

who name them):
good faithful father heron, I say,
who keeps the great
and lesser ticks
of my heart in place,
watching his messy family
of stars on the river,
that holding, that flow,
oh lovers,
that smear of moon
which never will clear
or clear up anything.

The Trail

Every day now
on waking
I walk down
the mountain
exactly
a mile,
over the
old trail
tramped
by a man
and his mule,
a miner
I'm told,
some dreamer
who failed,
going round
and round,
the snow
letting go,
giving way
to burnt gold
grasses
and brown
stones
unbending,
rolling,
the perfect

tracks
all slipping
their grips,
all losing
themselves
in the new
wash, this walk
we share
and share
again,
a rhythm,
a race,
almost
a religion
with no book,
no one
to lay on
the laurel,
the meaning,
no loud
exclamations,
a quiet
step
followed
by another,
a whistle,
a bird,

a little flick
of light
let loose
and falling
among
the gravel.

The Iowa Poetry Prize Winners

1987
Elton Glaser, *Tropical Depressions*
Michael Pettit, *Cardinal Points*

1988
Bill Knott, *Outremer*
Mary Ruefle, *The Adamant*

1989
Conrad Hilberry, *Sorting the Smoke*
Terese Svoboda, *Laughing Africa*

1993
Tom Andrews,
   The Hemophiliac's Motorcycle
Michael Heffernan, *Love's Answer*
John Wood, *In Primary Light*

1994
James McKean, *Tree of Heaven*
Bin Ramke, *Massacre of the Innocents*
Ed Roberson,
   Voices Cast Out to Talk Us In

1995
Ralph Burns, *Swamp Candles*
Maureen Seaton, *Furious Cooking*

1996
Pamela Alexander, *Inland*
Gary Gildner,
   The Bunker in the Parsley Fields
John Wood,
   The Gates of the Elect Kingdom

The Edwin Ford Piper Poetry Award Winners

1990
Philip Dacey,
   Night Shift at the Crucifix Factory
Lynda Hull, *Star Ledger*

1991
Greg Pape, *Sunflower Facing the Sun*
Walter Pavlich,
   Running near the End of the World

1992
Lola Haskins, *Hunger*
Katherine Soniat, *A Shared Life*